**Northamptonshire
County Council**
Libraries and Information Service

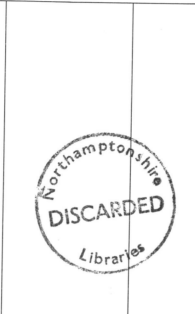

GOODMAN, P.

Plant classification

Please return or renew this item by the last date shown.
You may renew items (unless they have been requested
by another customer) by telephoning, writing to or calling
in at any library. 100% recycled paper   *BKS 1 (5/95)*

PLANT CLASSIFICATION

Polly Goodman

HODDER
Wayland

an imprint of Hodder Children's Books

Also in the series:
Animal Classification

Plant Classification is a simplified and updated version of Hodder Wayland's Classification: The Plant Kingdom

Text copyright © Hodder Wayland 2004
Volume copyright © Hodder Wayland 2004

Editor: Katie Sergeant
Designer: Simon Borrough
Typesetter: Jane Hawkins
Cover design: Hodder Children's Books

First published in 1999 by Wayland Publishers Ltd.
This edition updated and published in 2004 by
Hodder Wayland, an imprint of Hodder Children's
Books

British Library Cataloguing in Publication Data
Goodman, Polly
Plant Classification
1. Botany - Classification - Juvenile literature 2. Plant
diversity - Juvenile literature
I. Title
580.1'2
ISBN 0750245840

Printed and bound in China

Hodder Children's Books
A division of Hodder Headline Limited
338 Euston Road, London NW1 3BH

Cover: The bird of paradise flower (*Strelitzia reginae*) belongs to the banana family. Its brightly coloured petals resemble the plumage of flying birds of paradise.

Title page: North American pitcher plants (*Sarracenia purpurea*) are carnivorous. They have water-filled leaves that trap insects.

Below: A tree unfurling its new leaves is a sure sign that spring has come.

CONTENTS

The Kingdoms 4

Mosses and Liverworts 6

Horsetails 10

Ferns 12

Plants with Seeds 16

Conifers 18

Flowering Plants 22

Flowering Plant Diversity 28

Survival 34

Reproduction 42

The Future for Plants 44

Glossary 46

Finding Out More 47

Index 48

THE KINGDOMS

There are over 2 million types of living things in the world. To avoid confusion, scientists have sorted, or 'classified', them into groups according to their similarities and differences. New discoveries are being made all the time and added to the classification system.

Most scientists divide the entire living world into five groups, called kingdoms. These kingdoms are: animals, plants, fungi, protists and monerans. Each kingdom is divided into smaller and smaller groups, each of which have more features in common.

This book looks at five groups, or phyla, in the plant kingdom: mosses and liverworts, horsetails, ferns, conifers and flowering plants.

Each kingdom is divided into smaller and smaller groups: phyla, then (not shown) classes, orders, families, genera, and finally species. This diagram shows the phyla of the plant kingdom. ▶

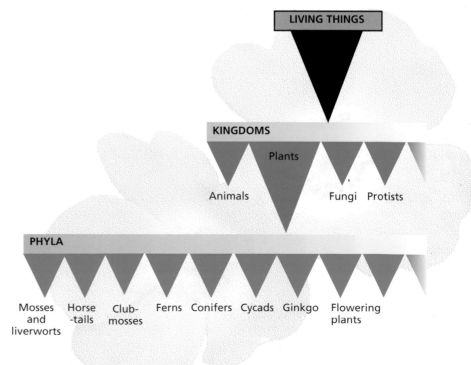

LIVING THINGS

KINGDOMS

Plants

Animals   Fungi Protists

PHYLA

Mosses   Horse   Club-   Ferns Conifers Cycads Ginkgo Flowering
and   -tails   mosses   plants
liverworts

Species

The smallest groups are called species. They contain living things that share two main characteristics: first, they look similar; and second, members of the same species can breed together in the wild. Sometimes two species of plants breed and produce young, called hybrids. However, the hybrids are often unable to produce young.

Names

Most familiar living things have a common name, such as 'oak' or 'poppy'. But there are 800 species of oak in the world, and 120 species of poppy. Also, common names of plants change in different languages. To help identify each species more accurately, in the eighteenth century, a Swedish scientist called Carolus Linnaeus (1707–78) gave all living things Latin names. Each species' Latin name is the same all over the world.

◄ This flower's common name is 'purple foxglove'. Its Latin name is *Digitalis purpurea*, meaning 'purple fingers'.

MOSSES AND LIVERWORTS

Mosses and liverworts are small plants that often grow in clumps. Instead of roots, slender growths, called rhizoids, anchor them into the soil. Most mosses and some liverworts have thin leaves, but liverworts usually have flat, rounded leaves.

The liverwort (*Marchantia polymorhpa*) was named after its flat, rounded leaves, which look a little like a liver.

Characteristics of mosses and liverworts

- often grow in clumps
- grow in damp places, such as rainforests, freshwater areas, and bogs
- spread by making spores
- absorb water and nutrients directly through their leaves
- have two distinct stages in their life cycle

Life cycle of mosses and liverworts

Mosses and liverworts do not have flowers or seeds. Instead, they reproduce and spread by producing spores, which are tiny, dust-like particles.

The life cycle of a moss or liverwort plant has two, very different stages. In the first stage, the green, leafy moss plant (gametophyte) grows male and female sex organs, which produce sex cells. The male sex cells swim through water on the surface of the plant and fertilise the female sex cells.

In the second stage, the fertilised cells grow into smaller plants called sporophytes. These produce capsules containing thousands of spores. The spores are released and spread by the wind or water, and they grow into new, leafy plants.

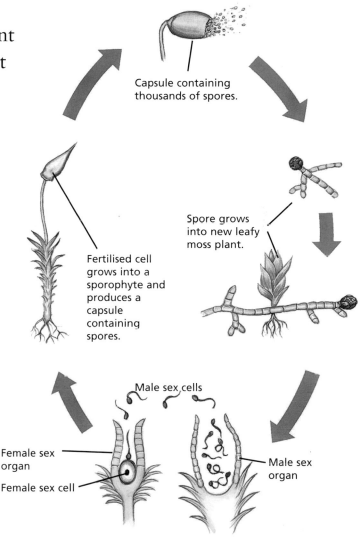

Capsule containing thousands of spores.

Spore grows into new leafy moss plant.

Fertilised cell grows into a sporophyte and produces a capsule containing spores.

Male sex cells

Female sex organ

Female sex cell

Male sex organ

▲ This diagram shows the two different stages in the life cycle of a moss or liverwort: the green, leafy plant and the sporophyte stage.

Habitat

Mosses and liverworts live in damp habitats such as tropical rainforests, wet, temperate forests, riverbanks and bogs. Since they have no real roots, they can grow on hard surfaces such as rock faces and walls.

Damp rocks sprayed by waterfalls are ideal places for mosses to live.

Food and water

Like all plants, mosses use sunlight to make their own food through photosynthesis (see page 35), but they also need water and nutrients. Unlike most plants, which take up water and nutrients through their roots, mosses and liverworts absorb water directly through their leaves.

With no water travelling through the plant, mosses and liverworts shrivel and dry out in hot weather, but they quickly recover after rain. In some dry places, the mosses will shrivel during the summer and start to grow again in the autumn.

▲This moss (*Polytrichum commune*) has reached its sporophyte stage. When the capsules are ripe, they will open and shake out the spores inside.

HORSETAILS

Horsetails are upright plants with rigid stems surrounded by rings of branches. About 300 million years ago, huge horsetail trees grew in vast, steaming swamps. Today there are under 30 smaller horsetail species. They are usually found in damp places, near rivers and lakes, or in swamps.

Rings of branches are growing from the stems of this horsetail (*Equisetum telmateia*). ▶

Characteristics of horsetails

- grow in damp places, such as near rivers and lakes, or in swamps
- rings of branches surround the stems
- spread by making spores
- water and nutrients travel from roots to stems and branches
- leaves are like tiny scales around the stems
- have two distinct stages in their life cycle

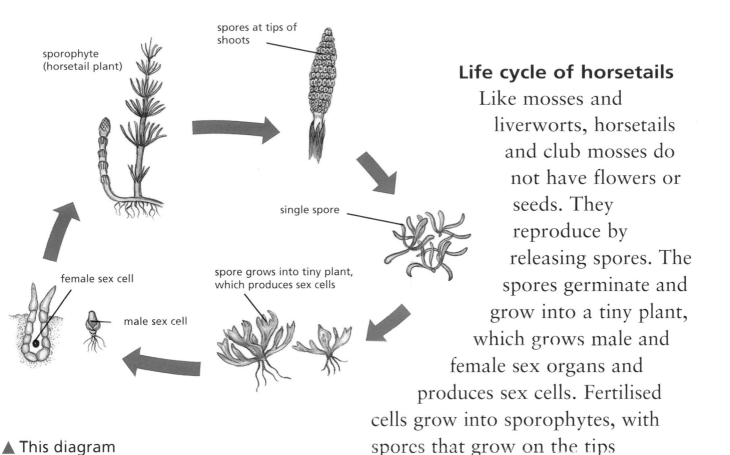

spores at tips of shoots

sporophyte (horsetail plant)

single spore

female sex cell

male sex cell

spore grows into tiny plant, which produces sex cells

▲ This diagram shows the life cycle of horsetails.

Life cycle of horsetails

Like mosses and liverworts, horsetails and club mosses do not have flowers or seeds. They reproduce by releasing spores. The spores germinate and grow into a tiny plant, which grows male and female sex organs and produces sex cells. Fertilised cells grow into sporophytes, with spores that grow on the tips of shoots.

Club mosses

Club mosses are not mosses, but relatives of horsetails. They are small plants with stems that trail along the ground, and tiny, needle-like leaves. The leaves grow in a spiral pattern around the stems. The first stage, or prothallus, of the club moss grows underground. It can take years to germinate and another fifteen years to produce sex cells.

Club mosses can form a carpet across the ground as their stems grow horizontally. ▶

FERNS

Ferns are green, non-flowering plants with long narrowing leaves. The leaves of many ferns are lacy and consist of hundreds of tiny leaflets. Ferns vary in size from small plants with leaves only a few centimetres long, to tall fern trees with leaves up to 6 metres long. The leaves are covered in a waxy coating to prevent them drying out.

Ferns have small roots anchored to an underground stem. The leaves grow from small buds at the base of the stem, inside which each leaf is tightly coiled. Each bud takes up to three years to develop. When it is fully grown, the bud unrolls and the leaflets rapidly open out.

Characteristics of ferns

- grow in damp, shady places, such as riverbanks and woodlands
- have green leaves that are tightly coiled at first
- spread by making spores, which grow in tiny capsules on the undersides of the leaves
- water and nutrients travel up the roots to and through the stems and leaves
- have two distinct stages in their life cycle

You can see the spore capsules growing on the underside of this leaf. The capsules are covered by tiny, protective flaps. ▶

◀ The leaves of this ostrich fern (*Matteuccia struthiopteris*) are fully grown and finally unfurling.

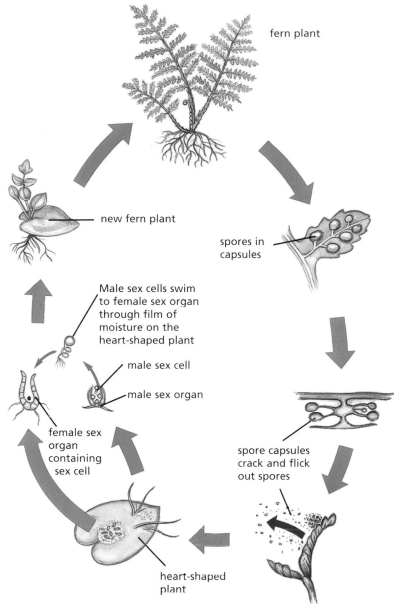

fern plant

spores in capsules

new fern plant

Male sex cells swim to female sex organ through film of moisture on the heart-shaped plant

male sex cell

male sex organ

female sex organ containing sex cell

spore capsules crack and flick out spores

heart-shaped plant

Life cycle of ferns

Spores grow inside tiny capsules on the underside of the leaves. When the capsule dries, it cracks and flicks out the ripe spores. Each spore germinates and grows into a tiny, heart-shaped plant, which grows sex organs and produces sex cells. Fertilised cells grow into a new fern plant.

◀ Simple blade

Habitat

Ferns depend on moisture to reproduce, so they grow best in damp, shady areas such as riverbanks and temperate woodlands. However, ferns can survive in drier climates than horsetails and mosses because of the waxy coating on their leaves which prevents water loss.

▲ Tripinnate leaf: blade is divided three times

Leaf shapes

There are about 12,000 species of fern in the world today, each with different shaped leaves. All leaves have a stalk, and one or more leaves. Simple leaves have a single blade. Others have leaves divided into leaflets, called pinnate leaves, or leaflets that are themselves divided, called bipinnate leaves.

◀ Pinnate leaf

▲ Palmate leaf: blade is divided like the fingers of a hand

◀ Bipinnate leaf

Types of fern

One of the most common types of fern around the world is
bracken, which is unpopular with farmers because it is
poisonous to livestock. Tree ferns (see page 44) grow in
tropics and other areas with warm climates. They have a
woody trunk with a crown of large fronds (leaves) at the top.
Filmy ferns have extremely thin, delicate fronds, which dry
out very easily. Filmy ferns only grow in tropical rainforests
or wet forests.

PLANTS WITH SEEDS

Mosses, liverworts, horsetails and ferns all reproduce by releasing spores. Other plants, such as conifers and flowering plants, reproduce by releasing seeds. Seeds are much bigger and more complex than spores. Each seed contains a tiny, young plant and a supply of food, covered in a protective shell.

What's the difference between seeds and spores?

SEEDS
- are made of many cells
- contain a tiny young plant
- carry food reserves
- are spread by wind, water, or animals

SPORES
- are made of one cell
- do not carry food reserves
- are carried, or spread, using wind or water

▲ Flowering plants cover a mountainside in Colorado, USA.

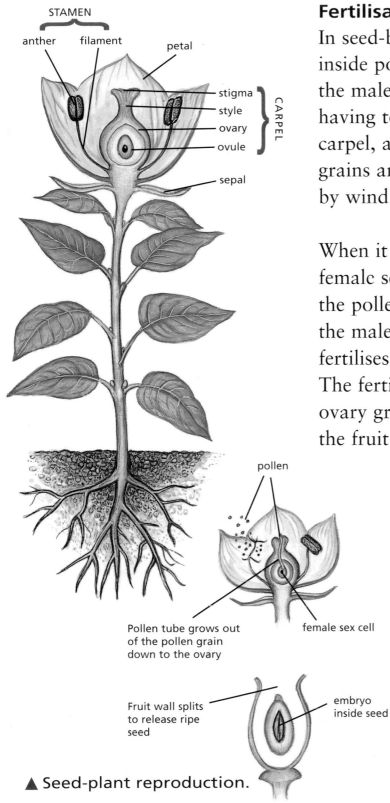

STAMEN
anther filament
petal
stigma
style
ovary
ovule
CARPEL
sepal

pollen

Pollen tube grows out
of the pollen grain
down to the ovary

female sex cell

Fruit wall splits
to release ripe
seed

embryo
inside seed

▲ **Seed-plant reproduction.**

Fertilisation

In seed-bearing plants, male sex cells grow inside pollen grains, which are produced in the male sex organ, or stamen. Instead of having to swim to the female sex organ, or carpel, as in spore-bearing plants, the pollen grains are carried to the female sex organ by wind or animals.

When it lands on the stigma, part of the female sex organ, a tiny tube grows out of the pollen grain down to the ovule. Then the male sex cell travels down the tube and fertilises the female sex cell in the ovule. The fertilised egg grows into a seed and the ovary grows into a fruit. When it is ripe, the fruit splits and releases the seed.

Since seed-bearing plants do not rely on water for fertilisation, they can live in more habitats than spore-bearing plants. This means they are more common.

CONIFERS

Conifers are trees or shrubs that grow seeds in woody cones. The word 'conifer' comes from the Latin word meaning 'cone-plant'. Most conifers are evergreen, which means they are leafy all year round.

Typical conifer trees have tall, straight trunks and narrow, symmetrical (regularly arranged) branches.

Characteristics of conifers

- tree or shrub
- leaves are sharp needles or tiny scales
- leaves are leathery, covered in a waxy outer layer
- most are evergreen (keep their leaves all year round)
- seeds grow in cones
- one main stage in their life cycle

Cones and seeds

Cones differ in size and appearance according to their sex and their species. Pollen grows on male cones, which are small and light. The pollen is carried by the wind to young female cones, which are larger, with soft scales.

Once the female cone has been fertilised, its scales close. The seeds grow inside it for up to three years. By this time the female cone is large and heavy and wood-like. When the weather is warm, the cone opens and releases seeds with thin, brown wings, which are carried away by the wind.

This branch shows male cones (small, pink cones), a young female cone (upright and pink) and a woody mature female cone. ▶

▲ Italian cypresses (*Cupressus sempervirens*) are tall and narrow. Like all cypresses, they grow well in warm climates, such as the Mediterranean.

Habitat and use of conifers

Conifers grow well in cool climates. Their tough, leathery leaves mean they can survive snow and frost, and they cover many of the world's mountainsides. In the northern hemisphere they often form dense forests, many of which are specially planted. Since they grow tall and fast, conifer timber is used as a building material or made into paper. In addition, millions of conifers are used as Christmas trees every year.

Species

There are about 520 species of conifers. They are divided into seven families, all of which have similar leaves and cones. Members of the pine family, which includes pines, firs, cedars, larches, and spruces, all have needle-like leaves. Yews also have needle-shaped leaves, but cypresses have small, scale-like leaves that cling to the stem.

Pines include some of the largest and toughest conifers. Their leaves give off a sweet smell. Yews have poisonous leaves, bark and seeds. Instead of cones, the seeds grow inside bright-red fleshy cups. Cypresses have round cones covered in shield-shaped scales. Their leaves give off a spicy smell.

The ginkgo tree is the oldest-surviving member of a group of trees growing at the time of the dinosaurs. It first grew in China, but is now planted in parks and gardens all over the world. It grows well in towns and cities and can survive in polluted air.

One of the strangest-looking conifers is the Chile pine. Its snake-like branches have given it the name 'monkey puzzle tree', because monkeys find it difficult to climb.

The fan-shaped leaves of the ginkgo tree (*Ginkgo biloba*) are exactly the same as those on trees living 150 million years ago. ▼

FLOWERING PLANTS

Flowering plants make up the largest group of plants in the plant kingdom. They grow in the form of trees, shrubs or herbaceous (soft-stemmed) plants. Flowering plants produce flowers, and seeds enclosed in fruits. The fruits vary from soft fleshy strawberries to hard acorns.

Common poppies (*Papavar rhoeas*) all flower at the same time on the edges of farmland in Europe. ▼

Characteristics of flowering plants

- can be trees, shrubs or herbaceous

- have roots, stems, leaves, flowers, and fruits

- have flowers made up of the sepal, petals, stamen and carpel (see page 17)

- the female sex cell, the ovule, is enclosed inside the ovary

- the seeds grow inside the ovary, which becomes the fruit

Annuals, biennials and perennials

Flowering plants live for different lengths of time, depending on whether they are annuals, biennnials or perennials.

Annuals are plants that grow, produce flowers and seeds, and die in a short time. This can be a few weeks or a few months.

Biennials are plants that take two summers to complete their life cycle. They grow leaves one summer, and flowers and seeds the next.

Perennial plants can live for many years. Herbaceous perennial plants grow flowering shoots in the spring, which die back in the autumn. Perennial trees and shrubs lose their leaves in the winter, but live off food stored in their woody stems or trunks until the spring. Flowering trees are known as 'broadleaved' trees to distinguish them from the needle-leaved coniferous trees. They can live for 300 years or more.

▲ The Pacific dogwood (*Cornus nuttalli*) is a shrub that grows white flowers every spring.

Habitat and use

Flowering plants grow all over the world, although most species grow in the tropics. They provide essential food for people, since most edible plants, including fruits, vegetables and grains are flowering plants. Flowering plants also provide beauty and scent.

Flowering plants are divided into two groups: dicotyledons and monocotyledons.

Characteristics of dicotyledons

- have two seed leaves
- the first root branches out into secondary roots
- herbaceous or wood-like
- broad leaves, often with a leaf stalk
- vascular tissues arranged in rings inside each stem
- leaves have a network of veins
- flower parts grow in multiples of four or five

Dicotyledons

Dicotyledons, or dicots, are the largest group of flowering plants. They include all broadleaved trees and many smaller plants. The seeds of a dicot sprout with two seed leaves. Microscopic channels called vascular tissues carry food and water around the plant. In a dicot, these tissues are arranged in a ring up the stem.

Vascular tissues in a dicotyledon are arranged in a ring inside the stem. ▼

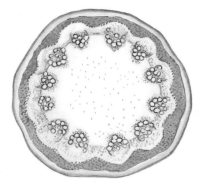

Vascular tissues in a monocotyledon are scattered throughout the stem. ▼

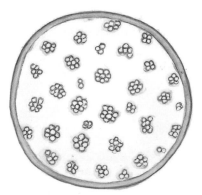

The dicotyledon flower

Parts of the dicot flower, such as the petals, grow in multiples of four or five. The outer sepals protect the flower when it is in bud. In some dicot species, they help to scatter the seeds. In flowers that are pollinated by insects, the petals are brightly coloured to attract the insects.

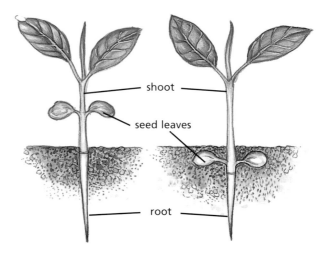

▲ Some dicots have seed leaves that stay below the ground, while others grow above the ground and turn green.

▲ The dog rose *(Rosa canina)* relies on insects to carry away its pollen, so its petals are brightly coloured.

Germination

All seeds need moisture, oxygen, and warmth to germinate. Some seeds germinate within a few days. Others stay dormant (inactive) for weeks or months until the conditions are right to germinate. When it is ready, the seed absorbs moisture from the soil, and food stored in the seed leaves passes to the embryo (young plant). A root grows down into the soil while a shoot grows upwards above the soil. When the seedling has grown leaves, germination is complete because the plant can make its own food.

Monocotyledons

Monocotyledons, or monocots, have seeds that sprout with a single seed leaf. They are mostly small or medium-sized herbaceous plants. A few, such as palms, look like trees. Grasses, orchids, daffodils and bananas are all monocotyledons.

Characteristics of monocotyledons

- have one seed leaf
- the first root dies and is replaced by a second root system
- mostly herbaceous
- vascular tissues are scattered throughout the stem
- long, narrow leaves without a stalk
- leaves have parallel veins
- flower parts grow in multiples of three

◄ Lily flower parts grow in multiples of three.

The monocotyledon flower

Monocots have flowers that grow in multiples of three. The leaves are usually narrow with parallel veins, and the vascular tissues are scattered throughout the stem (see diagram on page 24).

Orchids and palms

Some monocotyledon plants, such as lilies and orchids, have distinctive flowers. Orchids have a central petal that is very different in shape from the other petals. This petal is called the labellum, or lip. It may look like a trumpet or cup.

Most palms have a tall trunk with no branches, and a crown of leaves, or fronds. The fronds are usually feather or fan-shaped. Palms grow from a single bud in the centre of the crown. If this bud dies, the whole plant dies.

Many palms look like trees, but they are not true trees because they do not get thicker stems every year. This is because their vascular tissues are scattered throughout the stem, like all monocotyledons, instead of in rings inside the stem.

Date palms (*Phoenix dactylifera*) have been grown for over 3,000 years for their edible fruits, called dates. ▶

FLOWERING PLANT DIVERSITY

Flowering plants grow all over the world, but different parts of the world have very different species. This is due to the climate of an area, and the way the Earth's crust has moved over millions of years. The species that grow in an area, country or continent are called its flora. Species that grow naturally in an area are called 'native'. Species that have been carried there by people are called 'introduced'.

Holarctic
Paleotropical
Neotropical
Cape
Australian
Holantarctic

▲ This map shows the six main regions of different flora.

Worldwide

Some families of flowering plants, such as the buttercup family, grow all around the world.

▲ The creeping buttercup (*Ranunculus repens*) is native to Europe, Asia and Japan. It has been introduced to America and New Zealand.

Islands

Since islands are separated from the mainland, they often have very different species. Some islands have species that do not appear anywhere else on Earth. These species are called endemic. Most of the flora of the Hawaiian Islands is endemic.

Australia

Australia was separated from what is now Antarctica about 200 million years ago. As a result, its flora developed differently from other countries and it has many distinctive species. The eucalyptus, or gum tree, is native to Australia. There are about 600 different species that have adapted to habitats within Australia.

▲ The red-flowering gum (*Eucalyptus ficifolia*) was named after its red flowers.

Rainforests

Rainforests contain a larger diversity of native plants than any other habitat. The Amazon rainforest has tens of thousands of different plant species. These include trees, smaller flowering plants and climbers, as well as ferns, mosses and liverworts. This diversity makes rainforests extremely valuable.

Grasses

Grasses are the world's most widespread type of flowering plant. There are about 9,000 species, many of which provide essential food for people and animals. Rice, wheat and maize provide the basic food for most of the world's population. They are called cereal crops. Other cereal crops include rye, barley and oats.

Rye

Barley

Oats

Wheat

These cereal crops feed people and livestock. ▶

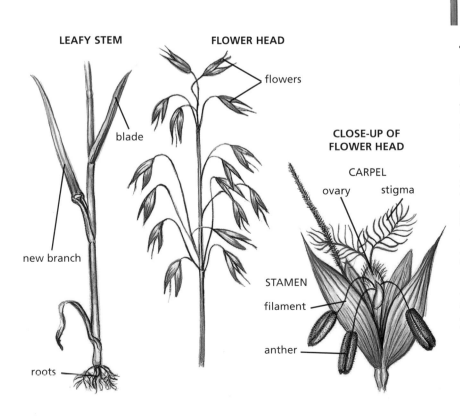

LEAFY STEM

FLOWER HEAD

flowers

blade

new branch

roots

CLOSE-UP OF FLOWER HEAD

CARPEL

ovary   stigma

STAMEN

filament

anther

The grass plant

Grass plants often grow close together to form a turf. New branches grow at ground level. A mass of tangled roots grows into a mat just below the ground. Grasses are wind-pollinated (see pages 42-43). Their flowers produce dusty pollen that causes hay fever in many people.

◀ These diagrams show the structure of a grass plant.

Grazing and mowing

Grass is able to survive being grazed by animals such as sheep and cattle, and mown by lawnmowers, because of the way it grows. New branches grow from buds at ground level. When the top of the plant is bitten or cut off, the buds are unharmed and the branches continue to grow. The leaves also grow from their base and continue to grow if the tops are removed. Grass will die if there are too many grazing animals in an area because they will eat the buds of the plant, as well as the leaves.

Bamboos

Bamboos are unusual types of grasses. They have hard, woody stems and can grow very tall. The giant bamboo (*Dendrocalamus giganteus*) can grow up to 35 metres high. People make the hard, hollow stems into cooking utensils, baskets and building materials.

◀ Pampas grass (*Cortaderia selloana*) has large white flower heads. It is a popular plant in gardens and landscaped areas.

Fruits and vegetables grown in
one country can be sold on the
other side of the world. ▶

Food

Fruit, vegetables
and cereal crops all
come from flowering
plants. People have
grown cereal crops
such as wheat, rice
and maize for
thousands of
years. In the past,
apples grew only
in Europe, bananas
grew in South-east
Asia, and potatoes grew
only in South America. Today these fruits and
vegetables are grown in many parts of the world.

The importance of flowering plants

Flowering plants provide us with food, clothing and
shelter, as well as many other products. Trees provide
wood for building, making furniture and other goods.
Paper is made from pulped wood. Cork, rubber, soap
and chewing gum all come from trees or palms.

Rubber and cotton

Rubber comes from the sap (a liquid within plants) of a tree that is native to Brazil. It is used to make tyres and other products. Most people wear clothing made from cotton. There are about 30 species of cotton plants, but most cotton fibre used for clothing comes from just one species, the *Gossypium* plant.

Drinks

Tea, coffee and hot chocolate all come from flowering plants. Tea is made from the leaves of the tea plant, which originally came from China. Coffee is made from the roasted seeds of coffee plants, which originally came from Africa. Chocolate is made from the cocoa plant, which comes from the Amazon rainforest.

Medicines

Many useful medicines come from plants. Some have been used for hundreds of years. The purple foxglove is used to make a drug called digoxin, which helps treat heart disease.

Cotton fibres in cotton plants are attached to the seeds in the fruit capsule. ▼

SURVIVAL

Like all living things, plants need certain essential elements to survive. They need sunshine, water, mineral nutrients and oxygen. They also need to be able to reproduce and spread out successfully.

This plant (*Welwitschia mirabilis*) grows in the dry Namibian Desert. It traps moisture using its long leaves. ▼

Photosynthesis

Plants need energy to survive, but instead of getting it from their food, like animals, they get it directly from the sun. This process is called photosynthesis. During photosynthesis, the leaves of a plant absorb sunlight. They also take up water from the roots and carbon dioxide from the air. They use the sunlight's energy to convert water and carbon dioxide into sugars. The sugars travel round the plant and are used for fuel or growth. Oxygen is produced as waste and goes into the air.

Oxygen is produced as a waste product.

Sunlight and carbon dioxide enter leaves.

Sugars are made during photosynthesis and travel around the plant.

Water passes up the stem to the leaves.

Water is absorbed by the roots.

Adaptation to habitat

Plants live in very different habitats. Some habitats lack water or sunlight, while others lack mineral nutrients. Over thousands of years, plants have adapted to the different habitats in order to survive. Different plants are suited to different habitats.

Forests and sunlight

In forests, lots of trees compete for light by growing as many leaves as possible. Beneath the trees it can be quite dark on the forest floor. Plants that grow here cope with the lack of light in different ways. In deciduous woodlands, where trees lose their leaves during winter, many smaller plants flower in the spring, before the trees have grown new leaves.

Wood anemones (*Anemone nemorosa*) flower in early spring, before the trees have grown their leaves. ▼

Climbing plants

In tropical rainforests, where the trees are evergreen and have their leaves all year round, smaller plants have to find other ways of getting to the light. Climbing plants, or vines, climb up tree trunks to reach the sunlight above the canopy (top layer of branches), where there is the most sunlight. Rattan palms climb trees using sharp hooks to dig into the trunks, while passion flowers have twisting, thread-like leaves called tendrils, which they wrap around twigs and branches to help them climb up.

Epiphytes

Some mosses, liverworts and ferns grow on branches of trees to get enough light. They are called epiphytes. They absorb water directly through their leaves or through their roots. Instead of reaching into the soil, epiphyte roots cling to the bark or dangle in the air.

▲ Many different epiphytes can cover a whole tree branch, bark or trunk.

On the forest floor, plants survive in very little light using specially adapted leaves. These leaves make the most of the light that reaches them. Plants that receive less light grow more slowly.

Like most cacti, this rainbow cactus (*Echinocereus pectinatus*) has spines instead of leaves. Apart from protecting it from animals, the thin spines reduce the amount of water lost from the plant because they have little surface area. ▶

Water

Plants that live in dry habitats, such as deserts, are adapted to survive without water for months or even years. Some plants have very long roots to reach moisture deep beneath the ground. Others, such as cacti, store water in thick stems.

Some desert plants survive mostly as seeds underground. When rain falls, the seeds quickly germinate, flower and produce new seeds, all within a few weeks.

Preventing evaporation

In rainforest canopies, rainwater evaporates quickly in the hot sun. Epiphytes have waxy leaves to stop moisture escaping. The leaves are shaped to funnel the water towards the centre of the plant. Sometimes the leaves store water at their base.

Aquatic plants

Plants that live in water do not have as much oxygen as other plants because they are partly submerged underwater. They have to get oxygen in special ways. Water lilies have air spaces in their stems, which trap oxygen above the water's surface. Mangrove trees live in shallow sea water along coasts. They have long breathing roots which stick up above the water to absorb oxygen.

The fringed water lily (*Nymphoides peltata*) lives in shallow lakes and ponds, with its roots anchored in the mud. ▶

Mineral nutrients

Apart from food and water, plants need mineral nutrients to survive. Mineral nutrients come from rocks and are dissolved in moisture in the soil. Plants absorb the nutrients through their roots, and carry them up through the stem to the leaves.

Minerals

Plants need six main minerals to survive:

- Nitrogen
- Phosphorus
- Potassium
- Calcium
- Magnesium
- Sulphur

They also need small amounts of other chemicals, such as iron, copper and zinc.

Fertile soils have lots of different minerals. They also have the broken-down bodies of dead plants and animals, called humus. In infertile soils, such as in bogs and swamps, some plants get their nutrients from insects that they trap instead. These plants are called carnivorous plants. The Venus fly trap (*Dionaea muscipula*) has spiny traps on each leaf, which snap shut when insects land on them.

The common sundew (*Drosera rotundifolia*) is a carnivorous plant that catches insects using its sticky leaves. ▶

All living things need nitrogen, but most plants cannot use the nitrogen gas that makes up about 78 per cent of the atmosphere. They need it to be combined with other elements by a special nitrogen-fixing bacteria. Some of these bacteria live in the soil, but others live in the roots of plants such as the pea family.

Some plants take all their food and water from another plant. They are called parasitic plants. The plant to which they attach themselves is called the host plant.

Broomrapes are parasitic plants. They attach themselves to the roots of another plant (their host), from which they get water and nutrition. ▶

REPRODUCTION

Many plants can reproduce in two ways. In one method, seeds or spores grow into a new plant. This is called sexual reproduction. In the other method, part of a plant, such as a stem, a leaf or a runner, grows into a completely new plant. This is called asexual, or vegetative, reproduction.

Strawberries reproduce using their runners. Roots extend out from the runners and grow into new plants. ▼

Pollination

In seed-bearing plants, male pollen travels to the female parts of a flower, or female cone, on insects or in the wind. Wind-pollinated flowers produce lots of dry, dusty pollen to maximise the chances of reaching its target. Insect-pollinated flowers attract insects with colourful petals and sweet scents.

Birds are attracted to flowers by their sweet nectar and brightly coloured flowers. ▶

Coconut seeds are covered in a thick, waterproof shell, which keeps the seed afloat so it can be washed ashore to germinate. ▼

Dispersal

Seeds need to spread out from the parent plant so the new seedlings do not compete for light and water. Most seeds have features that help them to be carried by the wind, animals, water, or people.

Some wind-pollinated plants, such as the sycamore, have fruits or seeds with wing-like structures to keep them in the air. Others, such as the dandelion, have fruits with fluffy coverings.

Many animal-pollinated plants have sweet, juicy fruit to tempt animals to eat them. The swallowed seeds pass out in the animals' droppings, far away from the parent plant. Some plants have fruits or seeds that cling to the fur of an animal using spines or sticky coats. Other seeds, such as geraniums, are dispersed when the fruit explodes, scattering the seeds in all directions.

THE FUTURE FOR PLANTS

There are millions of different species in the plant kingdom. This diversity is essential for humans and animals to live, since it provides food, medicines, shelter and materials. Yet thousands of plants are known to be in danger, or threatened with extinction.

Tree ferns are among many different plants in this tropical rainforest on the island of St Lucia, in the Caribbean. ▼

Rainforests help to make the earth livable by absorbing carbon dioxide from the atmosphere and releasing oxygen. They are also home to two-thirds of the world's plant species. But vast areas of rainforests disappear every year as populations grow and people clear land for farming.

The main dangers for plants today are the destruction of their habitat, the growth of cities and modern farming techniques. Conservationists are working hard to find ways of protecting the diversity of the plant kingdom from human development.

Botanical gardens

Botanical gardens help to protect endangered species as well as providing recreation for people interested in plants. The toromiro tree from Easter Island has been extinct since 1960. However, it has survived in botanical gardens around the world and there are now plans to reintroduce it back into the wild on Easter Island.

Genetic engineering

For hundreds of years, farmers have chosen to grow plants for certain features, such as their taste, or the size of their crop. More recently, scientists have been using a technique called genetic engineering, which alters the genetic material of a living thing to change its characteristics. Genetic engineering can be used to create a crop that is not harmed by herbicides, or that grows in a particular colour.

Genetically modified plants may be very important to the future of medicine, industry and agriculture. Yet some people are worried that not enough is known about genetic engineering to use it safely. There are concerns that it might damage people's health, or that it might harm the environment.

As scientists find out more about genetically modifying plants, it is essential that we protect the diversity of natural plants alive today, as well as their natural habitats, for future generations and the earth we live on.

Scientists are using genetic engineering to produce potatoes that are resistant to disease. ▼

GLOSSARY

canopy The top layer of branches in a forest that forms a roof-like canopy.

carnivorous Feeding mainly on other animals.

carpel The female sex organ of a flower, consisting of the stigma, style and ovary.

deciduous Shedding leaves each autumn.

diversity Variety.

dormant Inactive or sleeping.

embryo A living thing in the early stages of its development.

endemic Plants that are only found in a particular area.

evergreen Leafy all year round.

extinction Wiped out.

fertile Able to produce seeds and fruit.

fronds The leaves of a fern or palm.

gametophyte A stage in the life cycle of plants in which the sex cells are produced.

genetic engineering The scientific altering of genes or genetic material to change the characteristics of living things.

germinate To start to grow or sprout.

habitat The type of area where an animal or plant naturally lives.

herbaceous A plant with soft stems.

herbicide A chemical used to kill weeds.

introduced Species that have been taken to an area by people rather than growing there naturally.

leaflets Small leaves.

mineral nutrients Substances from minerals in the ground that provide nourishment for living things.

native A living thing that originated in the area where it is found.

nectar A sweet liquid produced by some flowers, which attracts insects and birds that carry out pollination.

perennial Live for a number of years.

photosynthesis The process used by plants to make food from carbon dioxide in the air and water from the soil.

pollination The process of carrying pollen between flowers for fertilisation.

seedling A young plant that grows from a seed.

sepal A leafy flap that protects the flower while it is still a bud.

sporophyte The second stage in the life cycle of mosses and liverworts.

stamen The male sex organ of a flower, consisting of the filament and anther.

temperate A climate that is neither very hot nor very cold.

tropics The region of the earth between the Tropic of Cancer and the Tropic of Capricorn.

FINDING OUT MORE

DK Nature Encyclopedia (Dorling Kindersley, 1998)

Junior Nature Guides: Mushrooms and Fungi/Trees/Wild Flowers (Chrysalis, 2003)

Life Cycles: Sunflowers and Other Flowering Plants by Sally Morgan (Chrysalis, 2001)

The Life of Plants: Classification/ Growth/Habitats/Parts/Reproduction/ Products by Louise & Richard Spilsbury (Heinemann, 2003)

Living Nature: Flowers by Angela Royston (Chrysalis, 2002)

Living Things: Adaptation/Classification/Survival and Change/Food Chains and Webs/Life Cycles/Cells and Systems by Anita Ganeri (Heinemann, 2001)

Looking at Plants: Flowers, Fruits and Seeds/People and Plants/Plants and Life/Roots, Stems and Leaves by Sally Morgan (Chrysalis, 2002)

Picture acknowledgements

Cover: Corbis (Alison Wright).
Inside: Bruce Coleman: title page (Marie Read), 5 (William S. Paton), 9 (P. Clement), 10 (Jeff Foott Productions), 13 (Hans Reinhard), 16 (John Shaw), 19 (Hans Reinhard), 22 (Allan G. Potts), 30 (Hans Reinhard), 31 (Harald Lange), 33 (Hans Reinhard), 34 (Dr Eckart Pott), 37 (Luiz Claudio Marigo), 38 (John Cancalosi), 41 (left/Kim Taylor), 41 (right/Goerge McCarthy), 42 (bottom/M. P. L. Fogden); Natural History Photo Library: 6 (Laurie Campbell), 11 (Jane Gifford), 12 (N. A. Callow), 18 (Eric Soder), 21 (Stephen Dalton), 25 (Laurie Campbell), 29 (right/Pavel German), 36 (Laurie Campbell), 39 (Hellio and Van Inden), 42 (top/G. I. Bernard); Oxford Scientific Films: 15 (David Fox), 26 (Deni Bown), 29 (left/Michael Leach), 43 (John Brown); Science Photo Library: 45 (Peter Menzel); Tony Stone: 8 (Terry Donnelly), 20 (Joe Cornish), 23 (Jack Dykinga); Wayland Picture Library: imprint page, 27 (Julia Waterlow), 32, 44.
Artwork: page 5 by Simon Borrough; all other artwork by Peter Bull Art Studio.

INDEX

animals 31, 35, 38, 40, 43
  food 30, 35, 44
aquatic plants 39

bamboos 31
bogs 6, 8, 40
botanical gardens 45
buds 12, 25, 27, 31

cacti 38
carnivorous plants 40
carpel 17, 23, 30
cereal crops 30, 32
climates 9, 14, 15, 20, 28
climbing plants 29, 37
cones 18, 19, 20, 21, 42
conifers 4, 16, 18-21
cotton 33

desert plants 34, 38

evaporation 39

ferns 4, 12-15, 16, 29, 37
fertilisation 7, 11, 17, 19
flowering plants 4, 16, 22-27
  diversity 28-33
flowers 7, 11, 22, 23, 26, 27, 30, 42
food
  humans 24, 30, 32, 44
forests 15, 20, 36, 37
fruit 17, 22, 23, 24, 27, 32, 43

genetic engineering 45
germination 11, 13, 25, 38
grasses 26, 30-31

habitats 17, 36, 38, 44, 45
  conifers 20
  ferns 14
  flowering plants 24, 28, 29
  horsetails 10
  mosses and liverworts 8
herbaceous plants 22, 23, 24, 26
horsetails 4, 10-11, 14, 16

leaves
  conifers 20, 21
  ferns 12, 13, 14
  flowering plants 24, 25, 26
  grasses 31
  mosses and liverworts 6, 9
life cycles
  conifers 18
  ferns 12, 13
  flowering plants 23
  horsetails 10, 11
  mosses and liverworts 6, 7
lilies 26, 27
liverworts 4, 6-9, 11, 16, 29, 37

medicines 33, 44, 45
minerals 34, 36, 40
mosses 4, 6-9, 11, 14, 16, 29, 37

nutrients 6, 9, 10, 12, 34, 36, 40

orchids 26, 27

palms 26, 27, 32, 37
parasitic plants 41
petals 23, 25, 27, 42
photosynthesis 9, 35
pines 20, 21
plant food 9, 24, 40, 41
  reserves 16, 23, 25
pollen grains 17, 19, 25, 30, 42
  tube 17
pollination 42
  animal 16, 17, 43
  insect 25, 42
  water 16
  wind 7, 16, 17, 19, 30, 42, 43

rainforests 6, 8, 15, 16, 17, 29, 33, 37, 39, 44
reproduction 7, 11, 14, 34, 42-43
roots 37, 39, 40, 41
  ferns 12
  flowering plants 24, 25, 26

grasses 30
horsetails 10
mosses and liverworts 6, 9
rubber 32, 33

seeds 7, 11, 16-21, 22, 23, 33, 38, 42
  dispersal 25, 43
  germination 43
  leaves 24, 25, 26
sex cells 7, 11, 13, 17, 23
soil 6, 25, 37, 40, 41
spores 6, 7, 9, 11, 12, 13, 16, 17, 42
stamen 17, 23, 30
sunlight 9, 35, 36, 37
swamps 10, 40

trees 10, 12, 20, 21, 22, 29, 32, 33, 36
  deciduous 36
  evergreen 18, 37
  trunks 15, 18, 23, 37

vegetables 24, 32

water 8, 10, 12, 17, 24, 34, 36, 38, 40
  absorption 6, 9, 35, 37
  dispersal 7, 43
  loss 14, 38-39
  store 38, 39
waxy coating 12, 14, 18, 39
woodlands 12, 14, 36